ICI PHOTOGRAPHY

AWARDS · 1992

ISBN 0 948489 1 1 1

The National Museum of Photography, Film & Television
is part of the National Museum of Science & Industry

Edited by Penny Fell

Designed by Imelda Kay
Typeset on Apple Macintosh in Gill Sans

Printed by Jolly & Barber, Rugby

NATIONAL MUSEUM
PHOTOGRAPHY · FILM · TELEVISION

PICTUREVILLE · BRADFORD

ICI PHOTOGRAPHY AWARDS
1992

FOREWORD BY COLIN FORD

WITH ESSAYS BY

DAVID BRITTAIN

AND

ANDREAS MULLER-POHLE

Sponsored by

FOREWORD

'A high-quality competition in which the very finest British photographers would be honoured to participate'. That was the declared objective of the National Museum of Photography, Film & Television's Sun Life Awards when they were launched in 1987. It was still the main aim of the second Awards competition and exhibition held in 1989.

Sponsors, photographers and Museum had every reason to be pleased with the achievements of 1987 and 1989. The winners of the first two Fox Talbot Prizes, Ron O'Donnell (1987) and Mari Mahr (1989) were genuine stars (they still are); the short list was almost equally distinguished (picking the winner was a close-run thing in both years); the other nominees made up a representative survey of the very best in British photography, in many modes. The National Museum of Photography's collection of contemporary work was considerably enhanced, and its audience introduced to the work of many fine photographers.

But we all wanted more. To show the pictures outside Bradford, perhaps even abroad. To make the Fox Talbot Prize attract as much attention to the medium of photography as the Booker Prize did to books, the Turner Prize to painting and sculpture, the Oscars to films. To widen the range of the types of photography included even further.

Now, the support of a new sponsor, ICI, makes us confident that we will achieve most of those ambitions. The 1992 entries will have been seen at the National Portrait Gallery, London, and the judges' short-list at Photokina, Cologne, before they arrive in Bradford; other touring venues will follow. And, most importantly, the Awards are no longer solely British. The new format adds a new ICI International Photography Prize to the Fox Talbot Prize; each is worth £10,000 to the winner. The sixty nominated photographers (thirty from Britain, thirty from the rest of Europe) each win £250. All in all, the prize money totals an impressive £35,000 - well worth competing for. In 1994, we plan to extend the Award to the Americas.

None of this could have been achieved without the generous and imaginative support of ICI. Having committed themselves to a dramatic uplift in funding the competition, they have also provided very considerable advice and practical help. Their European representatives have guided us through countries where the Museum has never worked before, and led us to new friends in all of them. We are deeply grateful.

We are also sincerely grateful to our old friends in the National Portrait Gallery, London. Having invited us to exhibit the entries in their galleries, they welcomed us with open arms. It is a great pleasure to be working with such professionals again, and to show the photographs in such a fine venue. Nor would our list of thanks be complete without two more inclusions. Firstly ABSA, whose generous award under the Business Sponsorship Incentive Scheme has enabled us to launch the 1992 Awards with such a flourish; and, secondly, the distinguished panel of judges who gathered in Bradford with the visually challenging task of picking the British and International winners for 1992. Theirs was a nearly impossible job: we cannot thank Kevin Byram, Gloria Chalmers, Bill Ewing, Mari Mahr, Michael Rand and Karl Steinorth enough.

Since their inception, the Awards have depended on the collaboration of those informed professionals who have nominated the photographers who especially interest them. This year, sixty of them, throughout Europe, have responded to our requests, championed their choices, and written about them, with an enthusiasm and promptness which we had no right to expect: the fax machine has penetrated deep into the heart of Eastern Europe, too! Finally, two editors of important and influential magazines have provided informed and revealing surveys of the state of European photography for this catalogue.

To all of them - sponsors, exhibitors, nominees, contributors - we give our heartfelt thanks. Most of all, we thank the photographers. It is they who have made the pictures, which are what the Awards are all about; they who fire all of us with enthusiasm; they who have made the work which will give pleasure to all who visit the exhibition, look at this catalogue, or see it in the National Museum's collection. *They* alone can ensure that photography never stands still. We salute them.

Colin Ford

Head of the National Museum of Photography, Film & Television, Chairman of the Judges

PHOTOGRAPHY IN BRITAIN

One role of such a major award as the National Museum of Photography, Film & Television's Fox Talbot Prize is surely to take regular stock of the shifting state of British photography.

What are the Prize's nominators looking for? 'Photography' means something different to everyone who uses a camera: the only factor which the nominated photographers have in common is that they live and work in Great Britain. A wide variety of talents, they are not all even photographers in any conventional sense. Their diverse pictures, frequently made for such art contexts as galleries, catalogues and books, can also be seen in colour magazines or editorial, on album covers or posters.

So what do we mean by 'British photography'? It is difficult to ascribe an identity to something so vague, especially in a time like the present, when global culture pervades and mingles with national culture, and hybrid art forms proliferate. But let us assume that there is some kind of consensus.

British photography has always been sustained by a sense of its own history and nature. As part of establishing art credentials for this relatively new medium, generations of commentators have linked it with the history of British painting, print-making and writing. They evoke the social concerns of Hogarth, Mayhew and Swift to explain the 'Britishness' of such documentarists as Bill Brandt, Chris Killip (nominated for the Fox Talbot Prize in 1987) and Martin Parr; they make the scientific nature of paintings by Turner and Constable the precedent for generations of landscape photographers, among them Roger Fenton, John Davies and Fay Godwin (the last two both nominees in 1987) and Raymond Moore. During the past decade or so, such views have seemed less satisfactory, seeming to exclude some photographers.

The face of British photography has changed dramatically during the twenty years or so in which it has received public subsidy. Complicated interactions - between photographers and funding agencies, educational institutions, galleries, publications, and the fledgling market in print sales -

have taken place against a background of enormous cultural and political upheaval and have been influenced by the complex debates of the post-Modernist era.

At the end of the 1960s, a strain of 'serious' art photography separated itself from amateur societies and commercial studios. Consisting of former art students, and fine art and documentary photographers, it looked to the USA for inspiration. Young Britons like Tony Ray-Jones travelled to New York, returning full of excitement; Antonioni's 1967 film *Blow Up* made it sexy to be a photographer; institutions such as The Photographers' Gallery and *Creative Camera* were established. That magazine's first editor, Bill Jay, has written about the high passions of those heady years, and the sense of naivety in discovery: 'Try to imagine this: you are desperate for photographic nourishment but live in a land where such food is non-existent.'

Since the '60s, two generations of photographers have emerged from the colleges to take advantage of the support structure of grants, galleries and publications. They include Martin Parr, whose irreverent colour documentary photographs inspired the making of a recent BBCtv series, *Signs of the Times*; Calum Colvin (a 1989 Fox Talbot Prize nominee), who constructs fantastic scenes from debris and rubbish; and the German-born Karen Knorr, with her mannered portraits of the English leisured classes. As I write, a third generation, with such photographers as Nick Waplington, is already knocking at the door.

Over the '70s and '80s, too, the 'closed club' that was British photography has opened its doors to many who are not strictly photographers in the pure sense. When the Surrealist, Man Ray, said that photography was not art, he was right in the sense that it has too many applications to be confined by any one orthodox practice. Photography permeates boundaries and invites radically different interpretations; this is what appeals to several groups of unconventional practitioners: artists who use mixed media and computers, sculptors, and assorted image scavengers, polemicists and theoreticians. These very different and diverse talents mean that there can be no such thing as British photography - only British 'photographies'.

A glance at any recent exhibition catalogue will reveal the sheer breadth of approach and methods. *Through the Looking Glass*, for instance, the Barbican's 1988 book on British post-war photography, contained work by individuals as diverse as Mari Mahr (who won the 1989 Fox Talbot Prize), Helen Chadwick (nominated in 1987) and Jo Spence (1987 and 1992), Bill Brandt and John Hilliard. This milestone survey replaced the orthodox history with a series of complementary historiographies or writings, each devoted to a different grouping of contemporary photography.

Through the Looking Glass recognised the importance of women's photography as well as the debt photographers owe to artists such as Richard Hamilton and Hamish Fulton; it celebrated the key role of foreigners settling in Britain (among them Kurt Hutton and Felix Man, both Germans who worked for *Picture Post* editor Stefan Lorant). But countless other historiographies or versions could have added a clearer picture of what British photography is today: one tracing the short history of Black photography, for example, or examining interactions between art photographers and the 1980s style magazines.

So the 1992 Fox Talbot Prize nominators have been able to select from a number of different traditions and opposing ideas of photography. The strand of fine art landscape is typified by the consummate black-and-white prints of Paul Hill and Thomas Joshua Cooper (a 1992 nominee); the strand of colour documentary (still the dominant British mode) includes John Kippin (nominated in 1992), Anna Fox (1989 and 1992) and Paul Reas (1992). One mainstream group, which includes Boyd Webb, Ron O'Donnell (winner of the 1987 Fox Talbot Prize) and David Griffiths, comes from fine art backgrounds to mingle photography with installation and appropriation; another includes Sunil Gupta (1989), David Hevey and Maud Sulter (1989), who use photography for polemics about representation or stereotyping.

Sometimes these strands cross-fertilise in fascinating and unlikely ways, as in the case of Martin Parr, who seems to be a conventional documentary photographer but actually explores some of that tradition's conceits and assumptions. Alternatively, they may exist in a state of mutual tension: gay or black artists often put themselves at odds with the dominant sources of photographic imagery in advertising, press or art photography.

Richly varied they may be, but the sources influencing British photography are far from ideal. Many argue that the cultural world undervalues photography, and that this is reflected in the relatively small sums of grant aid and sponsorship it attracts. Although our art support system is envied in many countries, including Germany, the funding of photography has its weaknesses. It does not help the wider public to understand the medium, and it obstructs efforts to integrate photography into a wider visual culture. Some argue that the institutions exist to benefit an élite, and that the system precludes anyone without privileged access to the channels of distribution. But no system is perfect and I believe that, if we cannot afford to be smug about 'British photography', we can certainly be proud of its achievements.

This discussion would be incomplete if it did not mention the many photographers and others who organise exhibitions and write catalogues mapping out this evolving story. We are fortunate that there are such informed people, able and willing to generate excitement about the medium. These are the kind of enthusiasts who have accepted the National Museum's challenge to select a representative sample of British talent for the ICI Photography Awards. In this sense, the Fox Talbot Prize is itself destined to become part of the fabric of British photography.

David Brittain

*(Editor of **Creative Camera**; freelance writer and broadcaster)*

EUROPEAN PHOTOGRAPHY

Europe is the theme for 1992: in Houston and Paris, Arles and Warsaw, everything revolves around European photography. But we are surely celebrating a political, rather than an aesthetic, event. If Europe is now a single huge sphere of communication, with a well-developed infrastructure and a supremely vigorous and productive photography, it does not have only *one* culture. We must take care not to seek one common denominator for all Europe. 'European photography' can only mean 'photography in Europe'.

When the publication *European Photography* first appeared early in 1980, the photography scene was divided mainly into regional movements, all more or less influenced by American photography. In retrospect, the renaissance of European art photography, from the mid-1970s on, was largely inspired by one American generation: Ralph Gibson, Les Krims, Lee Friedlander, Duane Michals and others. They represented the development of artistic traditions interrupted in Europe by national socialism and war (Otto Steinert's attempts to continue pre-war developments had failed in the 1950s). And we were beginning to realise that their ancestors were European pre-war achievements. In this respect, *European Photography* was intended as a manifesto: photography in Europe needed an awareness of its own existence, and a forum to present itself.

If there is little sense in making sweeping aesthetic statements about photography in Europe, it *is* worth comparing the situation of the countries of Western Europe with those in the East. In Spain, for instance, the restrictions of a totalitarian regime encouraged surrealism, no longer a force elsewhere in Western Europe, to survive into the 1980s. It faded away only on the death of Franco's fascism. How much more radically must the contours of photography in Eastern European countries - closed totalitarian societies, isolated not only from the West, but often also from their immediate neighbours - be re-drawn?

In the 1980s, despite fundamental structural differences between Eastern and Western Europe, both areas saw the revival of a kind of photographer who became the dominant figure of that decade. Known in French as 'auteur', in German as 'Autor' and in English as 'independent photographer' (and increasingly 'author'), this figure has two main characteristics:

Ethically, the independent photographer strives to be creatively self-determining, responsible only to himself - unlike the applied (or commercial) photographers who, paid to work for clients, can be responsible only for the formally technical quality of their work. In the West, independent photographers sought to be disassociated from the commercial marketplace; in the East, it was the State from which they sought dissociation.

Aesthetically, the independent photographer is concerned to shape a personal vision, striving for a distinctive trademark, style and artistic identity. These are not the goals of a commercial photographer or a state-subsidised artist, both of whom must accept the aesthetic criteria of their patrons.

In the West, 'auteurs' renounced the standards of advertising photography, setting harsh black-and-white against its gaudy colours; graininess against sharpness and detail; contemplative melancholy against frivolity. And in the East, there were - alongside direct services to State and Party - the `areas of freedom' which the independent photographer was supposed to avoid, aesthetic niches informally tolerated because in them collective self-control functioned best; the notorious salon nude photography became a trademark of this sort of Eastern freedom.

In the West, independent photographers clamoured for state help to escape the marketplace. While the Berlin photographer Michael Schmidt unsuccessfully demanded the salary of 'a middle-ranking civil servant', Norwegian photo-artists persuaded the government to give them grants for life. No less bizarre, a Dutch photo-magazine with 580 subscribers obtained state subsidies of 360,000 guilders per annum. In the East, photographers pinned their hopes on a free market: there was no such thing. Such customer institutions as there were - public collections and state-funded publications - were rarely politically neutral.

When the dams broke in the East, some photographers took the West by storm (with Miro Svolík, Tono Stano and other Czechoslovakian 'expressionists' being the most successful). Some were turned into monuments to resistance (a popular practice in Germany).

Up to this point, the model of independent or author photography had more or less developed in the aesthetic context of 'straight photography'. Now, new forms of photographic production came into force during the 1980s - directorial, staged, constructive forms which often resulted in garish, expressive works presented in giant formats and unusual settings. Compared with these, the imagery of the 'straight independents' seemed pale and unprepossessing. The old 'personal visions', once so exciting, suddenly became a jumble of documentary and subjectivity, merging in so general a style that it became almost impossible to recognise the mark of individuals. As a movement, author's photography lost its driving force; it became redundant.

In the mid-80s, a paradigm shift took place from photography by authors to photography by artists. Everything became suitable material for staging: object, subject, apparatus, and finally the picture itself - the most radical attack on the very idea of authorship.

The best and worst that culture had to offer was mercilessly grabbed and re-processed - trivia, rubbish, pornography, kitsch, fine art. The post-Conceptual, post-Modernist artists gave photography tremendous vitality, and integrated it into new artistic contexts such as installation art. Photographs, either as prints or as projected pictures, assumed a dominant role, leaping out at the viewer from the walls, becoming part of a multi-dimensional sculpture.

The shift from the paradigm of the 'author' to that of the 'artist' widened the interest to all kinds of cultural manifestation, whatever its creator, its place in the cultural hierarchy, or its inter-media relationships. Photography thus acquired a new dimension, in which aesthetic, political and technological strategies all connect. One can construct a model of this new photography, recognising the aesthetic dimension ('high' vs 'low' art), the political dimension ('left' vs 'right') and the technological ('digital' vs 'analog' photography).

Aesthetically, the battle between high and low art, itself not new, forms one of today's central aesthetic impulses, a reaction against automation and the search for technical perfection. An example is what I call the 'aesthetisation of waste'; the re-charging of fag-ends of information with new perceptual qualities. Fritz Vogel (of Zurich) takes scraps of photographs ('ready-mades') and collates them into signed artist's editions; Joachim Schmid (Berlin) assembles 'masterpieces of photographic art' in the form of snaps which strikingly resemble their originals; Keith Arnatt photographs objects he finds on rubbish dumps as metaphorical 'sculptures'. All these artists suggest that what we despise as waste can be surprising, informative, valuable, aesthetically rich. In contrast, they find the products of technological perfection redundant, ordinary and aesthetically impoverished; it is these products that belong on the rubbish dump. Thus, all our values are re-evaluated.

Politically aware photography is usually confined to Britain and North America, though there are signs of growing politicisation elsewhere, notably in Scandinavia. Alongside the inherited strategies of political art (Victor Burgin, Hans Haacke, Klaus Staeck and others), the most interesting new movements aim less at art galleries than at the street, and use the media of the street - posters, handbills, fly-sheets, T-shirts. Seeking to generate a new public, their work is often spectacular and unexpected. Such 'cultural activists' (a term coined by Douglas Crimp) operate in big city jungles, mostly in anonymous collectives (the Guerilla Girls, Gran Fury, Boys with Arms Akimbo). Their reactions to Aids, racism, sexism and war are succinct, illustrated with hard fact.

The cultural activists, too, are torn between the aesthetic intention to interpret and experience the world and the political intention to change it: an aesthetically rich (connotative) work is politically poor (denotative), and *vice versa*. But, while the traditional spaces of politics, street and market, are vanishing, and politics arrive as electronic entertainment in our private homes, the cultural activists aim at re-charging the political arena by aesthetic means, knowing that the political meaning of a message arises primarily from its context and its channel, and not from its aesthetic structure.

Technologically, photography is based on the idea of light threads connecting object and image. We instinctively feel this connection to be analogous ('logical' and 'rational') because it matches what we see with our own eyes. This natural state is now being eroded by digital machines. The analog threads are being chopped into computer bits, re-computed, disappearing into black holes of zero information in order to allow a new space to appear - an artificial, simulated, virtual space; a space without material objects or artefacts, but one of social processes between humans and the machines they have programmed. In Jeffrey Shaw's 'virtual museum', for example, one sits in a chair equipped with sensors to 'move' through video galleries. The direction of real and simulated movements is determined by turning and tilting the chair, and the visitor has experiences which contradict his or her own knowledge of the world: small rooms, for instance, contain larger rooms.

Finally, in experimental *Cyberspace*, this separation of the observer from the observed is completely abolished, allowing the spectator to dive into a mental world, an immeasurable holographic landscape in which limitations of time and space seem to disappear.

In the face of this technological revolution, classical divisions of reality and fiction, truth and illusion, collapse. So does the traditional idea of photography itself. When photography falls into the digital maelstrom, it will lose its uniqueness and become part of a global ensemble, the communicative basis of which - the digital code - promises to offer what photography always hoped to be, but never became: a truly universal world language.

Andreas Müller-Pohle

Photographer, Editor **European Photography**

FOX TALBOT PRIZE

PHOTOGRAPHS FROM
GREAT BRITAIN

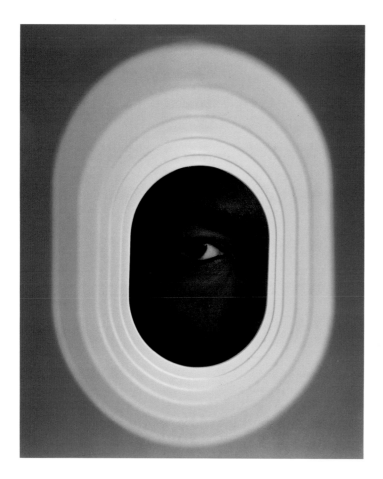

DAVE LEWIS

"**Dave Lewis chooses to document issues that are specific to Black communities. Through his particular lyrical style of constructed images, he will pull no punches. Underneath this stylised form of image-making lies an artist who is prepared to confront and challenge prejudice. He can be both brutal and sensitive in his reflections on the world.**"

Nominator: Mark Sealy, Autograph

PAUL REAS

"I think Paul Reas' essay on the British Heritage Industry makes very
pertinent points, in an appropriately plastic aesthetic, about the
revamped but tired remains of what was once grand British industry.
I am also very interested in the direction of his more recent work."

Nominator: Michael Collins, **Daily Telegraph Magazine**

3

THOMAS JOSHUA COOPER

"Tom Cooper's work is fascinatingly paradoxical.
Sometimes, one is enticed by its Victorian landscape
resonances, and sometimes by its rigorous minimalism,
where gesture overrides detail (as in his recent seascapes.)
But underlying everything for me is a consistency of vision
that marks him out as one of the most influential and
imaginative photographers over the last twenty years."

Nominator: Paul Hill

JANUSZ OLSZEWSKI

"Looking at his work, I feel like Alice in Wonderland - on the surface is a vibrant and exciting abandon of colour inviting the imagination to come out and play. Yet, exploring further, there are clues and hints which clearly indicate hidden messages of a more profound nature."

Nominator: Amanda Nevill, Royal Photographic Society, Bath

JO SPENCE

"Nominating Jo whilst she was still alive, I suppose I hoped she would use the award with typical pragmatism and humour. Now she's not here, it seems even more key to 'make official' the real importance of a woman who mud-wrestled with those most slippery and scary issues of class and the body politic. She could share ideas about Lacan, love, Foucault, sandwiches and death, and make you laugh. For me, that's about as important as image-making."

Nominator: Beryl Graham

TOM WOOD

"The everyday nightmare of using public transport has provided Tom with the opportunity to explore issues at the very heart of photography. There is so much to look at in his images. I would urge the viewer to look again and again. There are moments where accident and artifice collide. The images are a semiotician's dream."

Nominator: Dave Williams,
Open Eye Gallery, Liverpool

KEITH ARNATT

"For me, photographs become most intriguing and powerful when they simultaneously affirm and deny their most intrinsic quality. A photograph must be of something that exists in the world. Arnatt's pictures are pictures of beer cans, but cans that become convincing parodies of German Romantic paintings - they are credible fictions that dissuade us from our acceptance of 'truth' contained within them."

Nominator: David Hurn

 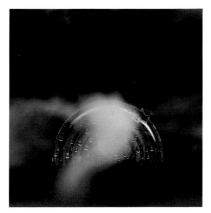 

OWEN LOGAN

"Owen Logan does not simply take elegantly crafted, eloquently constructed images, he also understands how to link one image to the next to create, in this case, two convergent, resonant and highly articulate sequences, one documenting Italians in Italy, the other their emigré cousins in Scotland. The pictures selected for this competition are all from the former sequence. They represent merely one melody from a complex sonata form."

Nominator: Alasdair Foster, Fotofeis, Edinburgh

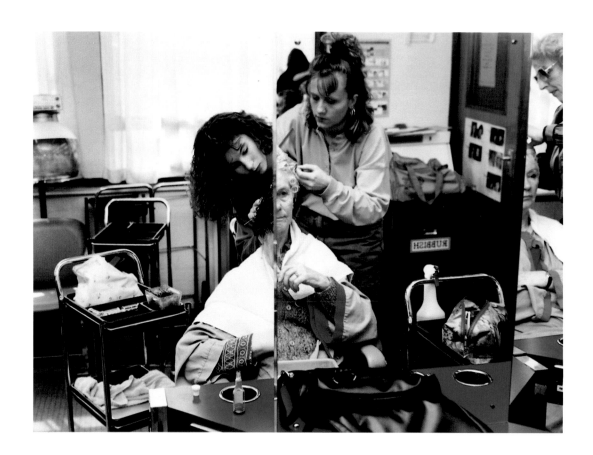

MALCOLM GLOVER

"Malcolm Glover's photographs strike me as an artistic body of work because his photographic baggage includes psychological perception and psychological intimacy. These qualities lift his pictures out of the sphere of journalism and place them amongst the best artistic work being done in Britain today."

Nominator: Raghubir Singh

DEBORAH WEINREB

"Of the many young
photographers it has
been my privilege to
meet, Deborah Weinreb
is the most original. She
has tried to find new
approaches to her
medium by using light
changes, an attempt at
three-dimensional
presentation, and fresh
materials. She is
undaunted by the
traditional and unafraid
of the new. She
is worthy of support."

Nominator: Eve Arnold

TRACEY HOLLAND

"Tracey Holland has moved into photography from a fine art background which goes some way to explaining the origins of her layered, almost 'old masterly' tableaux of selected and found objects. She arranges her pieces with the intuition and skill of an alchemist - with results which are at once quite exquisite yet disturbingly eerie."

Nominator: Wendy Hughes, Untitled Gallery, Sheffield

MIKE ABRAHAMS

"I have long admired Mike Abrahams, in particular his versatility and ability to work under difficult circumstances. His sensitive approach to the subject is the key to his highly individualistic personal style."

Nominator: Colin Jacobson, Independent Magazine

 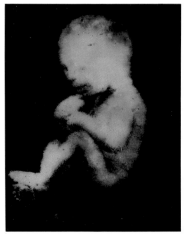 

PETER MAX KANDHOLA

"I think it's important that prestigious competitions such as the Fox Talbot Prize should not be completely dominated by the obvious big names of contemporary British photography. Peter is a young, highly talented, hugely energetic character and his eclectic approach, both in terms of subject and technique, helps confound the conventional expectations of what a young Black British photographer should be."

Nominator: Derek Bishton, Ten-8

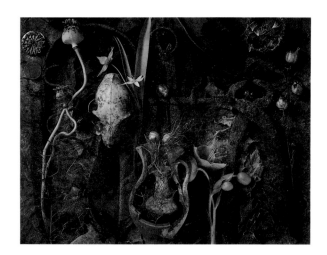

WINNER
FOX TALBOT PRIZE

JOHN BLAKEMORE

"John Blakemore is one of the most consistently creative artists working in photography, and his Garden series, made in 1990/91, explores magical inner landscapes of great resonance. His recent book *Inscape* is a long, long overdue celebration of his work."

Nominator: Fay Godwin

14

RONNIE SCOTT SIMPSON

"This occasion seemed to lend itself to putting forward a lesser known but highly individual young photographer whose dedication to the art of photography is paramount. Ronnie Scott Simpson is still pushing at the barriers of photography and using its qualities as a two-dimensional surface to explore and develop ideas. I have great admiration for his perseverance and realisation of images."

Nominator: Zelda Cheatle

ANNA FOX

"I first encountered Anna in 1983 when she was still
a student. She stood out so obviously from the
others. I like her approach - she takes on thorny
issues and treats them in an off-key way, bringing
to them humour and perception."

Nominator: Amanda Hopkinson

STEVE PYKE

"Steve Pyke's photographs are topographies, whether of the human face, the landscape or the street. Like many artists - from Rembrandt to Avedon - he details the physical surface as a mirror of the spirit beneath. His 'Philosophers' series is a monument to twentieth century intellect and reveals a commitment and intelligence rare in recent creative photography."

Nominator: Robin Gibson, National Portrait Gallery

(opposite)

THE DOUGLAS BROTHERS

"Why the Douglas Brothers? No simple answer. A feeling that they are deeply intrigued by their subject matter and their medium. The images resonate with this combination of a search for the heart of their subject and a seemingly casual technique which belies a constant experimental exploration of form.   If this sounds like 'artspeak', just look at the pictures."

Nominator: Philippe Garner, Sotheby's

KLANGER & BOINK INC

"Klanger and Boink come across as a breath of
fresh air in a very competitive area of the market.
Their approach isn't deadly serious: it is fun, tongue
in cheek, very colourful and a little kitsch. Their
pictures stand out a mile."

Nominator: Terry Hope, **Amateur Photographer**

MELANIE FRIEND

"Melanie Friend reports on what she sees thoughtfully and responsibly. Her photographs go beyond the obvious without being gimmicky or brash. In the best tradition of documentary photography, she has a sense of what makes a significant picture - whether it be humanity, newsworthiness or apposite comment."

Nominator: Maggie Murray, Format Photographers

JOHN KIPPIN

"John Kippin is a photographer living and working in the North East - the traditional heartland of Britain's 'social documentary' movement. Kippin deals with serious contemporary issues - yet he opts for a consciously constructed approach that denies the easy solutions of 'objective' black-and-white documentary photography."

Nominator: David Brittain, **Creative Camera**

HIDDEN
NATIONAL PARK NORTHUMBERLAND

LEN GRANT

"Len Grant's pictures are founded on a simple premise, all too often missing in contemporary documentary photography: he has a positive liking of people and a genuine interest in their lives. A strong urge to find out more, and a desire to pass on that information, makes for photographs which are accessible to as wide an audience as possible."

Nominator: Graham Marsden, Viewpoint Gallery, Salford

DAVID WILLIAMS

"David Williams' work is intense and reflective. His current photography explores the active interrelation of sequenced pictures. The recent series, Is : Ecstasies I - XXII, tackles a mystical idea through the reductive abstraction of unspecific images. He is presently moving into more dramatic and overt territory, proposing an installed landscape which surrounds and involves the viewer in the photographer's psychological 'reality' ".

Nominator: Richard Calvocoressi, Scottish National Gallery of Modern Art

ROGER HUTCHINGS

"Roger Hutchings is a very concerned photojournalist, perhaps one of the most concerned I have come across, and his photographs are improving all the time. There's a consistency in his work. He simply has a very good journalistic eye."

Nominator: Eamonn McCabe,
The Guardian

JULIAN GERMAIN

"Julian Germain has redefined the boundaries of documentary photography by including in his work photographs from many other sources. His willingness to place amateur photographs with his own images acknowledges the importance of family portraits in contemporary photography. By choosing Julian Germain, I have also chosen the millions who only take photographs on family occasions."

Nominator: Paul Wombell, Impressions Gallery, York

'Some things you forget, Other things you never do.'

"'She is a friend of my mind. The pieces I am, she gathers them and gives them back to me in all the right order'... that must mean that nothing ever dies "

ROSHINI KEMPADOO

"Roshini's current work is created by means of the new digital technologies and uses the familiar codes and conventions of our popular culture. However, her images powerfully convey fresh meanings and feelings that speak of her personal experiences - of family strengths, of travel and up-rooting, and of British racism."

Nominator: Barry Lane, Arts Council of Great Britain

JOHN FERRARA

"John is primarily a 'people photographer'. His approach is based on his ability to identify with his subject and to focus on one element, which he then develops to produce a sympathetic and graphic statement. He is equally skilled at using the available elements on location, and creating from scratch in the studio."

Nominator: David Lindsay, McCann Erickson Advertising

PETER FRASER

"Peter Fraser has contributed significantly to photographic culture. His work is innovative, constantly challenging and constantly revealing. He has constructed a language of colour which intimates a broad emotional and intellectual response and he has established a photography of ideas that is both distinct and new."

Nominator: Dewi Lewis, Cornerhouse, Manchester

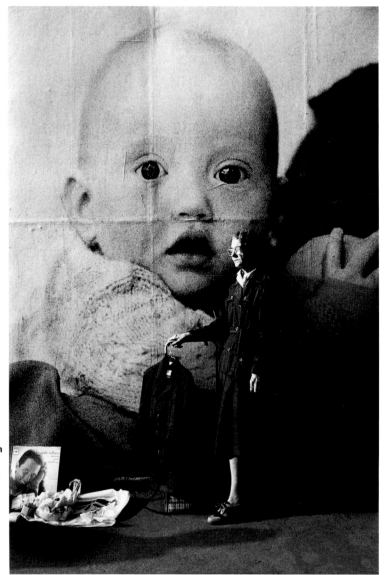

MARKETA LUSKACOVA

"Markéta Luskačová's direct, sympathetic and uncontrived pictures could only have been taken by someone blessed with patience, determination and integrity. What more can one ask of a photographer of people? Well, as Chris Killip has suggested, you can also have love. That shines out from these pictures, too."

Nominator: Sue Grayson Ford, The Photographers' Gallery

ROBIN GRIERSON

"There is a lot of tripe talked about contemporary British photography and, some would argue, there is a lot of tripe about in contemporary British photography. I admire the work of Rob Grierson for what it is: good, honest, compassionate photojournalism. Grierson documents what he cares about."

Nominator: Chris Dickie,
British Journal of Photography

ICI INTERNATIONAL PRIZE

PHOTOGRAPHS
FROM EUROPE

JOSEF KOUDELKA

"From the moment we opened up his boxes, we knew that a great image-maker was upon us. It was apparent that he, Josef Koudelka, had everything: all the qualities of the eye and heart, an ability to make himself accepted, an ease for being forgotten, a certain iron structure, a sense of curiosity, a vitality, an energy - giving his photographs enormous effectiveness."

Nominator: Robert Delpire,
Centre National de la Photographie, Paris

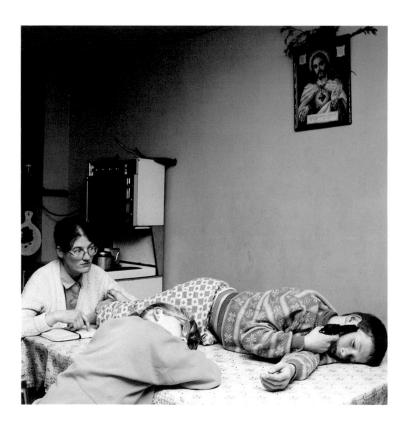

ANTHONY HAUGHEY

"I selected Anthony Haughey because when I first saw
his portfolio it struck me as not only an original body of
work for so young a photographer but one which
exploited the peculiarities of colour photography. In its
addressing of social and political issues, it also gives a
penetrating insight into the changing values in
contemporary Irish life."

Nominator: Christine Redmond, Irish Gallery of Photography, Dublin

FIN SERCK-HANSSEN

"Whether the pictures are about our environment, about the order of natural history, about existential or psychological problems - that is left to the viewer. But the pictures contain drama and humour and they arouse both curiosity and disgust (who likes stuffed birds anyway?) with their wonderful, ambiguous expressions."

Nominator: Robert Meyer, Institutt for Fotografi, Bergen

34

(opposite)

DIETER APPELT

"With a subtle balance of intellectual depth and personal aesthetics, Dieter Appelt uses the photographic medium to explore issues such as memory, time, death and the tension between nature and culture, defining some of the trends of contemporary *zeitgeist*."

Nominator: Joan Fontcuberta, Barcelona

35

AIVARS LIEPINS

"Aivars Liepins is a photo-reporter who fascinates not only with bare facts. He also explores inner processes where inner tensions find expression."

Nominator: Peteris Korsaks, Latvian Photography Museum, Riga

MIA LOCKMAN-LUNDGREN

"Mia Lockman-Lundgren's photographs cannot really be compared with any other current trend in contemporary pictorial art: her images leads us directly to an apocalyptic world which many artists seek to recreate but few can evoke with authenticity."

Nominator: Henning Hansen, Katalog, Odense

ANDRZEJ LACHOWICZ

"In recent years, Lachowicz has revived his earliest ideas, using old negatives and photo-montage to create 'artificial reality'. It is a form of self-quotation, not merely repetition of an old standpoint. These works try to synthesise intellectual and sensual tendencies and represent an important voice in present art discourse".

Nominator: Adam Sobota, National Museum, Warsaw

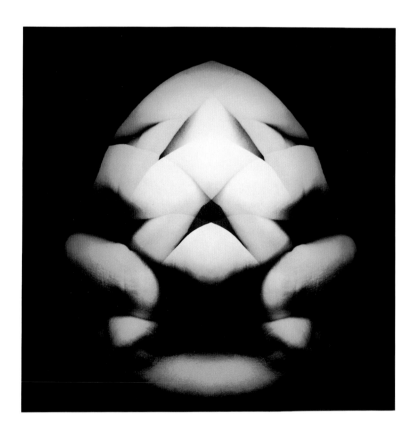

GABRIEL CUALLADO

"Gabriel Cualladó's photographs reflect his experience of life. He has not had to search for dramatic subjects or famous people; his work is concerned with everyday scenes, with friends or relatives. He is part of that group of photographers who embrace the words of Robert Frank 'I must express, without fear, my feelings about the world to which I belong.' "

Nominator: Josep Vicent Monzó, Instituto Valenciano de Arto Moderno, Valencia

WINNER
ICI INTERNATIONAL PRIZE

ROBERTO KOCH

"I thought highly of **Roberto Koch** ever since seeing his first works on social issues, like his project on disabled people in **Rome**. As he runs a photographic agency, it would be easier for him to shoot more commercial, remunerative images; he chooses other subjects. I hold him in esteem, not only as a photographer, but for his humanity."

Nominator: Gianni Berengo Gardin, Milan

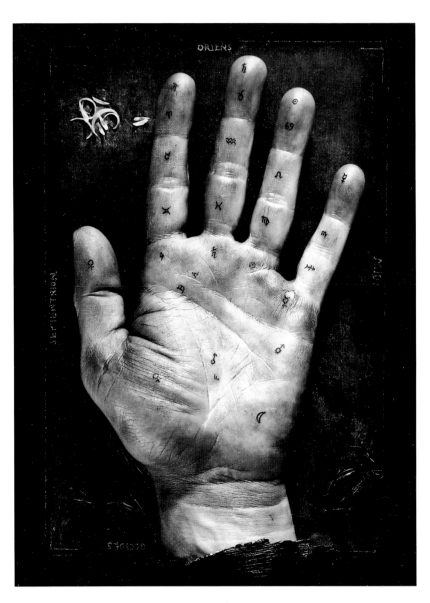

GABOR KEREKES

"I think Gábor Kerekes is a brave photographer: he dares to take photographs of seemingly uninteresting, everyday subjects. He does not manipulate what he sees but neverthless we see visions in his pictures. These are the images of a person who thinks and feels deeply, and passionately wishes to show the inner meaning of his world."

Nominator: Péter Korniss, Budapest

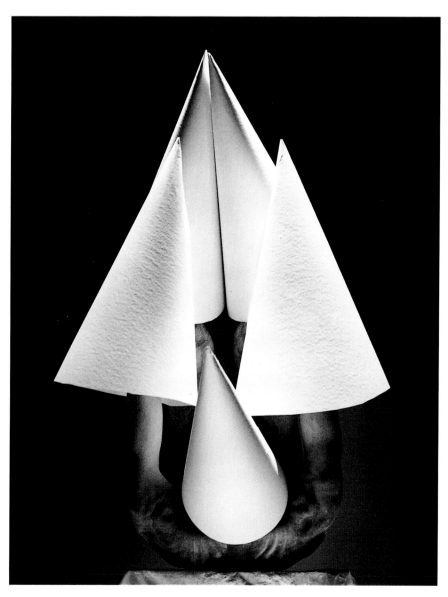

TONO STANO

"Tono Stano is the leader of a new wave of young Czechoslovakian photographers representing the body in motion as a visual expression of feeling, in a post-modernist style. His figures evolve in abstract space, reinterpreting reality, with a strong sense of composition."

Nominator: Anna Fárová, Prague

ALFRED SEILAND

"Precise composition, magnificent lighting, the captivating quality of his prints - these are only the obvious props in Alfred Seiland's photography. Mr Seiland is a quiet observer who presents us with reality in its various facets."

Nominator: Hans-Georg Pospischil, Frankfurter Allgemeine Magazin

MARINA COX

" She questions the reality of the photographic image, revisiting history with
a tongue-in-cheek sense of humour. I am also attracted by the formal
quality of Cox's work. Composed and printed in a masterly way, her images
have a dreamlike quality which reinforces the ambiguity of their content."

*Nominator: Alain D'Hooghe, **Clichés Magazine**, Brussels*

MIRO SVOLIK

"Miro enters the world of constructed photography with something very special, unique, fresh: he employs a playful and humorous vein of Czech art tradition....in his pictures there is a special mixture of joy, poetry, wisdom, humour, mystification, mystery. Miro makes this sad world more pleasant, or better: more acceptable. I see no other photographer who could do it."

Nominator: Daniela Mrázková,
Fotografie*, Prague*

A CROSS — COUNTRY RUN

3/3/1991 BRADFORD   The only picture of Miss Suzan Scott's kidnapping.   Γιώργος Δεπόλλας

YIORGOS DEPOLLAS

"The imaginary and the real - although these terms suggest two diametrically opposed approaches to photography, they need not bring about a division. Both may be contained in a photograph and co-exist in individual unity. Depóllas reproduces reality humorously and ironically, the real dissolving into the imaginary, and the imaginary becoming real, thus reconciling the image as object and the image as content."

Nominator: Stavros Moressopoulos, Hellenic Centre for Photography, Athens

GERARD UFERAS

"Gerard Uferas follows in the tradition of a Salgado or a Koudelka; his work attempts to illuminate reality, penetrating the illusion of surface appearances. In 1988, he began his vast fresco of Europe's Opera Houses behind the scenes, fascinated by the hidden activity that takes place there. His photographs show his affection for the detail of everyday life and his boundless passion for music and its mysteries."

Nominator: Jean Luc Monterosso, Paris Audiovisuel

EDOUARD BOUBAT

"Over the years, Edouard Boubat has depicted the Parisians with tenderness and love - and with a poet's eye. There is a formal strength and a unique impressionistic quality in his images of everyday life in the streets of Paris."

Nominator: Rune Hassner, Hasselblad Centre, Gothenburg

JACQUES SONCK

"I have been well acquainted with Jacques Sonck's work for more than fifteen years ... his portrait pictures are real social documents and have been compared, not without reason, with the work of Sander and Arbus. But he has evolved his own personal style, and his technical skills are highly accomplished."

Nominator: Roger Coenen,
Provinciaale Museum voor Fotografie, Antwerp

JORGE MOLDER

"The photographic works of Jorge Molder evince, above all, the silence of isolation. In this, they are exceptionally effective. They therefore point to the contemplation of the acts of choice upon which every photograph is necessarily predicated."

Nominator: Manuel Costa Cabral,
Centro de Arte e Comunicação Visual, Lisbon

AD VAN DENDEREN

"The photographs of Ad van Denderen inspire silence, curiosity - and ultimately a feeling of shame. You thought you knew the subject, but had never before looked as closely as he. In spite of the uncompromising quality of his black-and-white medium, his visual message is extraordinary for its subtle shades of meaning."

Nominator: Els Barents, Rijksdienst Beeldende Kunst, The Hague

GYORGY TOTH

"Despite its dispassionate quality, Gyorgy Toth's work reveals great sensitivity towards social problems. His new psychological portraits show an ambivalence between subject and photographer: this works as a kind of vivisection, though the model is always a close friend with whom he feels deep sympathy and empathy."

Nominator: Katalin Neray, Mucsarnok, Budapest

TUIJA LINDSTROM

"Tuija Lindström has developed a mature style of her own, but she can still surprise you. Photography seems to be a part of her so that she sees the beauty, or inborn stories, in everyday objects, and knows how to present these sights for others to discover."

Nominator: Ritva Tähtinen, Photographic Museum of Finland, Helsinki

PAUL DEN HOLLANDER

**"From the moment that he finished his photographic
studies in Breda, Paul den Hollander proved himself
able to approach reality, poetically. For twenty
years, he has transmitted this vision to others and
renewed it in a richly varied and coherent way."**

Nominator: Jan Coppens, Art Academy, Breda

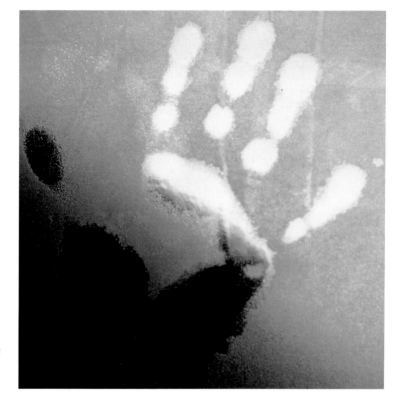

GIOVANNI GASTEL

"When he is not exploited by various fashion stylists or editors for commissioned images, Giovanni Gastel is, for me, one of the most creative and imaginative photographers. His education, as one of a noble family, his culture, his passion for the arts and his involvement, for some years, in the work of his uncle, Luchino Visconti, has made him one of the most culturally gifted photographers."

Nominator: Lanfranco Colombo,
Il Diaframma, Milan

(opposite)

KJELL STEN TOLLEFSEN

"It's not the large panoramas, portraits, news coverage that make his messages unique, but rather his ability to find hidden messages through significant details....The picture presented here is a typical example of his work, a picture, incidentally, that wasn't planned at all beforehand. A perfect visual display of 'Apartheid' in all its symbolic simplicity."

Nominator: Leif Preus, Preus Fotomuseum, Horten, Norway

LUC CHESSEX

"His photographs are a documentary record of humanity taken with respect and sense of personal involvement rarely found today. He travels the countries of the third world, photographing with total commitment. He sees photo-journalism as a way of making people think, never as a means of achieving the sensational photograph: this is his greatest strength."

Nominator: Erika Billeter, Museum of Fine Arts, St Legier

STEFAN MOSES

"One of the most interesting and important photographers in post-war Germany, his whole body of work deals with a single subject: the Germans. His recent project has been a portrayal of East Germans, in all sections of society: of all the many portfolios I have seen on this subject, his work is the most impressive because of its humanity."

Nominator: Christiane Gehner, **Merian***, Hamburg*

SERGEI GITMAN

"The night-long rally in Tbilisi marked the anniversary of the massacre of peaceful demonstrators by tanks, bullets and gas. Sergei Gitman's images of that rally epitomise the despair, the pain, the rediscovered sense of unity, and the determination to defy and end the age of communist repression."

Nominator: Andrei Baskakov, Russian Union of Art Photographers, Moscow

NADEZDA CHIPEVA

"A person of independent thinking, high moral integrity and professionalism, Nadezda Chipeva is creating politically unbiased photographic records of Bulgaria's transition from totalitarianism to democracy. She courageously creates a mosaic of objective images, uninfluenced by the policies of the day."

Nominator: Ivo Hadjimishev, Bulgaria

NIKOS ECONOMOPOULOS

"As an independent photographer, he chose to devote his recent years to an 'in depth' study of the sufferings of populations under repression which, in certain areas of the Balkans, has called for 'ethnic cleansing'. This work is very much in the tradition of concerned social documentary photography, towards a visual understanding of our society to which he has committed himself both physically and economically."

Nominator: James Fox, Magnum Photographers, Paris

THE PHOTOGRAPHS

AND

THE PHOTOGRAPHERS

1

DAVE LEWIS

From **Images of Emotion - Black Youth and Mental Health**

Cibachrome, 508mm x 610mm

Dave Lewis studied at the Polytechnic of Central London from 1982-85. Here, he was strongly influenced by 'issue-based' photography and his own constructed images explored being black and British. After graduating, he became a member of the black photographic group, D-Max, and from 1986-90, he worked on the **Blackfriars Photography Project**, documenting changes in the docklands of London. He currently works as a freelance photographer and educationalist.

2

PAUL REAS

From **Flogging a Dead Horse - the Heritage Industry and its Role in Post-Industrial Britain**

Colour, 508mm x 610mm

Born in Bradford in 1955, Paul Reas is a freelance photographer. One of the school of British social documentary photographers working in colour, he has exhibited throughout Britain and widely in Europe. His first major publication was *I Can Help* (1988); a recent long-term project has been the photographic study of a British family throughout a whole year.

3

THOMAS JOSHUA COOPER

Harbour near true North, the Great Orme, Gwynedd, North Wales, 1992

One of a diptych, Black-and-white/silver, 575mm x 400mm

Born in California in 1946, Cooper studied for an MA in Photography at the University of New Mexico and moved to Scotland in 1983, where he is Head of the Photography Department at Glasgow School of Art. He found inspiration in the British landscape and his photographs reveal and evoke 'a veneration for place'. He has exhibited regularly in the USA, France and Britain since 1971, and his work is held in many collections, including the National Gallery of Canada, Ottawa, the Victoria & Albert Museum, London and the Bibliothèque Nationale, Paris.

4

JANUSZ OLSZEWSKI

Roots

From the series **Landscape at the end of the 20th Century**

Colour, 560mm x 685mm

Born in Poland in 1954, Janusz Olszewski moved to London in 1981. His imaginative and striking work has attracted increasing attention in the last decade. He has exhibited at the Centre National de la Photographie, Paris; and the Royal Photographic Society and The Photographers' Gallery. His work is in the collections of the Victoria & Albert Museum, London and the Bibliothèque Nationale, Paris.

5

JO SPENCE

Epic Journey

From the series **Cancer Sequence** (unfinished 1992)

Colour montage, 1055mm x 902mm

Photographer, writer and photo-therapist, Jo Spence began her photographic career as a commercial portrait photographer. Political conviction compelled her to abandon this for documentary photography. She became well-known and respected for her radical work, founding Half Moon Photography Workshop and *Camerawork* magazine with Terry Dennett. She edited/wrote six books on photography and was a pioneer of both photo-therapy and photo-theatre. Jo Spence died in June 1992, shortly after her nomination for the Fox Talbot Prize.

7

KEITH ARNATT

Canned Sunsets

Colour, 178mm x 178mm each

Born in Oxford in 1930, Keith Arnatt combined teaching with photography until leaving Higher Education in 1990. He has exhibited at the Victoria & Albert and Tate Galleries, and at the Barbican Centre; his work has been shown widely abroad. In 1991, he won the Brandt Award.

6

TOM WOOD

Snowdrop Street, Stanley Road, Kirkdale, 1990

Scotland Road, Vauxhall, 1990

From **Liverpool Bus Series (A567 route)**

Colour prints, 432mm x 286mm

Irish-born, Tom Wood started working life as an Income Tax officer. He subsequently enrolled as a student of photography and film at Leicester Polytechnic. He now works chiefly in Merseyside and the North West and has exhibited at the Open Eye Gallery, Liverpool and at The Photographers' Gallery. His book *Looking for Love* was published in 1990.

8

OWEN LOGAN

The Procession

The Draw

From **The Links in a Chain**

Black-and-white/silver, 241mm x 241mm each

Born in 1963, Owen Logan left school at sixteen to become a freelance photographer. From 1979, he travelled widely, photographing in India, Greece, Morocco and Italy. His Italian work was the subject of a British Council Touring Exhibition and, in 1992, he received a Scottish Arts Council Documentary Commission to work with the Italian community in Scotland.

9

MALCOLM GLOVER

Oxford Street, London
From **The Self Image**

Colour, 508mm x 406mm

A documentary photographer, Malcolm Glover studied photography at Newport College and at the Royal College of Art. He has undertaken commissions on subjects as varied as rural Welsh life and Parkhurst Prison's Rehabilitation Centre. He has taught and exhibited widely and his current interest in the modern pre-occupation with **Self-Image** led to his 1991/2 exhibition of the same name. He was the 1991 *Sunday Times* Award Winner.

10

DEBORAH WEINREB

Future? August 1991

Installation, acetate projection print, 736mm x 1067mm

Born in London in 1960, Deborah Weinreb first used a darkroom whilst she was a student of bookbinding. She travelled widely in India and China before opting for a career in photography, and enrolling at the Polytechnic of Central London. Her commitment is to pushing out the boundaries of photography and challenging the ways it is viewed and used. She has worked with Eve Arnold for some years, and exhibits frequently in London.

11

TRACEY HOLLAND

From **Endgame** series

Colour, 915mm x 915mm

Tracey Holland was born in 1961. Initially a painter, she incorporates many media, including collage, into her work. Over the past four years, she has made increasing use of colour photography. She has exhibited frequently in the UK, including three one-woman shows. She lives and works in Sheffield.

12

MICHAEL ABRAHAMS

Shoot Out
From **British Suburban Cowboys**

Black-and-white/silver, 254mm x 254mm

Michael Abrahams is a founder member of the Network Photographers' Picture Agency. Born in Johannesburg in 1952, he studied at the Polytechnic of Central London and has worked as a photojournalist since 1975. His work was shown in the exhibition **Network in Eastern Europe** in 1990, and he is a frequent contributor to *The Sunday Times*, *The Observer* and *The Independent Magazine*.

13

PETER MAX KANDHOLA

Fragments from the Soul I, II & III

Colour triptych, 790mm x 990mm each

A career in Design Engineering preceded Peter Max Kandhola's entry into the world of photography, and his mixed media photographic work draws on technical expertise and experience. In 1991, Kandhola opened a new arts venue, The Goate Gallery in Birmingham; and in 1992, he was director of the city's first Photo Festival.

14

JOHN BLAKEMORE

From The Garden - Fragments of a History

Black-and-white/silver triptych, 406mm x 305mm each

John Blakemore has been a significant talent on the British photographic scene for nearly thirty years. His first one-man exhibition was in 1964: his major one-man shows, including **Still Life** and **Beyond Landscape**, have toured widely at home and abroad. In 1992, he was awarded the British Council Travel Fellowship.

15

RONNIE SCOTT SIMPSON

Untitled

Black-and-white/silver, 508mm x 610mm

Ronnie Scott Simpson graduated from the Royal College of Art as recently as 1990. He experiments with both black-and-white and colour, using photography as a medium rather than a lens-based format. He has exhibited with the British Council and at the South Bank Photo Show.

16

ANNA FOX

Paintball Marshall
From **Shot Away**

Colour, 508mm x 610mm

Anna Fox graduated in photography from West Surrey College of Art & Design where she now teaches part-time. Her project and book *Work Stations*, a study of corporatism and office hierarchy in the Thatcher years, first brought her work to the public eye. Anna Fox has exhibited widely in the UK and Europe; her most recent study **Shot Away** is about adult war games.

17

STEVE PYKE

Jacques Derrida
From **Philosophers**

Black-and-white/silver, 1181mm x 1105mm

Steve Pyke is a portrait photographer based in London. His chief project in 1990-92 has been to photograph the leading philosophers of the Western world. His individual black-and-white portrait style has attracted international attention: his work is in seven major collections, including the National Museum of Photography, Film & Television and the National Portrait Gallery.

18

THE DOUGLAS BROTHERS

Daniel Day Lewis

Black-and-white/silver, 305mm x 406mm

The Douglas Brothers were born, nine years apart, in Southend. Andrew Douglas gave his younger brother, Stuart, his first camera when he was nine. They grew up to study fine art and photography, respectively, and joined forces professionally in 1986 - one of the earliest of the photographic duos. Together they have won a cult reputation for exceptional, grainy, black-and-white portraiture.

19

KLANGER & BOINK INC

Alone on the Beach Watching Lovers at Night
The Critic
Couple in Café
From **The Desire to Sin Visually**, August 1991

Colour triptych, 508mm x 610mm each

Paul Jeff and Elizabeth McDonough met at Derbyshire College of Higher Education and formed a partnership on graduating, dividing their time between commercial and creative photography. Working increasingly in the fashion and pop industries, they have continued to explore themes of 'woman as an image', and representations of sexuality on many levels.

20

MELANIE FRIEND

The Wall, East Berlin, 5 January 1990

Black-and-white/silver, 305mm x 406mm

Melanie Friend studied English at the University of York and started taking pictures some years after graduating. In 1983, she joined Simon Guttman's Report agency and later joined Format agency. Meanwhile, she studied for a degree in photography at the Polytechnic of Central London. She has contributed to *The Independent* and *The Guardian*, and has undertaken major projects in Eastern Europe.

21

JOHN KIPPIN

Hidden (National Park, Northumberland)

Colour and text, 1715mm x1422mm

Born and brought up in the North East, John Kippin finds his photographic inspiration in the region. Using large-format, constructed images, his work is in sharp contrast to traditional documentary photography. He has exhibited in Britain and the USA and teaches photography at the University of Northumbria at Newcastle.

22

LEN GRANT

From **Salford's New Era - Faces of Change**

Black-and-white/silver, 280mm x 381mm

Len Grant started life as a sales executive, but turned freelance photographer in 1990, chiefly photographing people, and specialising in architectural and commercial work. He has undertaken two major projects in 1991/2, documenting social change in Salford and Manchester.

23

DAVID WILLIAMS

Ama et Fac Quod Vis. 1992
(Love and do as you wish - Augustine)

Black-and-white/silver triptych and text, 1105mm x 650mm

Once a songwriter, David Williams is now Head of Photography at Edinburgh College of Art. He has undertaken several major commissions and exhibitions including **Pictures from No Man's Land** which toured England and France in the 1980s. He relishes a description of his photography as 'a blues photographer, celebrating life as a package of inextricably-linked ups and downs'.

24

ROGER HUTCHINGS

A man abandons his home and flees from a sabotaged ammunition dump in Addis Abbaba
From **Victims of War**

Colour, 406mm x 305mm

A member of Network Photographers, Roger Hutchings studied documentary photography at Newport College of Art from 1980-82. He has worked since then as a freelance photo-reporter, documenting social and political issues around the world.

25

JULIAN GERMAIN

From Charles Snelling

Installation, colour prints shown, 737mm x 1067mm

Born in London, Julian Germain studied at Trent Polytechnic, Nottingham and at the Royal College of Art. A photographer and lecturer, his recent projects include the exhibitions **Steel Works** and **Ashford and Folkestone**, part of the Cross Channel Photographic Mission. He has exhibited in Britain, Europe and America.

26

ROSHINI KEMPADOO

From the series **With Our Spirit Companions**

Cibachrome photographs from computer-generated transparencies, 425mm x 590mm

Roshini Kempadoo took an MA degree in Photographic Studies at Derbyshire College of Higher Education in 1989. Exploring issue-based photography, and using computer-generated images, she examines the experience of being a black woman in a British culture. In a varied career, she has lectured, acted as consultant, worked as a freelance photographer, mounted six one-woman exhibitions, and contributed to many more.

27

JOHN FERRARA

Man with Flowers

Black-and-white/silver, 508mm x 406mm

John Ferrara was born in Italy and moved to Britain at the age of six. He became a chef but, after a year in the kitchens of the Savoy, turned to photography. As a freelance photographer he worked for *Nova*, *The Times*, *The Observer Magazine* and *Radio Times*. Since 1980, he has run his own studio, specialising in black-and-white advertising and editorial work.

28

PETER FRASER

Untitled 1990 (Swiss Alps)

Courtesy of Interim Art, London
Colour 1500mm x 1500mm

Born in Cardiff in 1953, Peter Fraser became convinced as he grew up that photography shared with established art forms 'the potential to express the fullest range of human spirit'. From the 1980s, he has had seven solo exhibitions, including **Everyday Icons.** He also lectures at Newport College of Art and Nottingham Polytechnic.

29

MARKETA LUSKACOVA

Woman selling a jacket, Bethnal Green Road, 1990

Black-and-white/silver, 406mm x 508mm

Born in Prague, Markéta Luskačová arrived in Britain in 1975 with an Arts Council Award to photograph in the North East. She has worked chiefly in the UK ever since. Her documentary work has included several projects photographing children and she has exhibited at the Victoria & Albert Museum; the Museum of Modern Art, Oxford; and the Bethnal Green Museum of Childhood, London.

30

ROBIN GRIERSON

Rubber tapper woman with child, Acre, Brazil

From Rubber Tappers of the Amazon

Black-and-white/silver, 508mm x 406mm

Durham-born, Robin Grierson studied photography at West Surrey College of Art & Design and the Royal College of Art. A documentary photographer, he works mainly for newspapers and has exhibited in Spain, Brazil and the UK.

JOSEF KOUDELKA

Untitled

Black-and-white/silver, 150mm x 470mm

Born in Moravia in 1938, Koudelka left Czechoslovakia in 1970 and became a British resident, moving later to France. His arrival on the photographic scene in Western Europe caused an immediate stir. His theatrical, expressive style put him in the forefront of contemporary photography. He has exhibited in the USA and Europe - including one-man shows at the Museum of Modern Art, New York; the Hayward Gallery, London - and the National Museum of Photography, Film & Television, Bradford.

32

ANTHONY HAUGHEY

From the series Home

Colour, 485mm x 480mm

Frustrated by factory work, Anthony Haughey turned to photography as a means of personal expression in 1986. He graduated from the West Surrey College of Art and Design in 1990. He works on social-based and political issues in colour and has exhibited in his native Ireland, Britain, France and Canada. His work is in the Centre Regional de le Photographie, Calais and the Victoria & Albert Museum, London.

33

FIN SERCK-HANSSEN

Untitled

Colour, 1250mm x 1250mm

After studying photography in Derby, England, Fin Serck-Hanssen returned to his native Norway in 1984 to establish a reputation for his individual style of constructed photography. He has exhibited extensively throughout Norway, and his work has been shown at the ICA, London and in the USA.

34

DIETER APPELT

Out Sequence, Siemens-Projekt

Black-and-white/silver, 437mm x 347mm

Dieter Appelt was born in 1935 and originally studied music in Liepzig and Berlin. In his mid-twenties, he started to study photography, with a special interest in experimental work. He has enjoyed an international reputation for many years and has exhibited extensively all over Europe, and at the International Museum of Photography in New York.

35

AIVARS LIEPINS

President of the Latvian Universal Stock Exchange, Janis Valters, Riga, Latvia, April 1992

Black-and-white/silver, 305mm x 465mm

Aivars Liepins was born in Riga in 1953 and has worked as a photo-journalist since 1977, acting as staff photographer for several Latvian magazines and newpapers. In 1991, with three other photographers, he set up Latvia's first independent picture news agency, AFI.

36

MIA LOCKMAN-LUNDGREN

Cro-Magnon Dreams

Polaroid to negative, printed on Melanex, 500mm x 475mm

Born in 1963, Mia Lockman-Lundgren lives and works in Gothenburg. She entered the School of Photography at the University of Gothenburg in 1987. She developed a personal style of creative photography, using experimental techniques, and has exhibited in Sweden and Denmark. In 1992, she won the University of Gothenburg's grant for artistic development.

37

ANDRZEJ LACHOWICZ

Topologie, 1991

Printed on canvas, 1100mm x 1100mm

Born in Wilno in 1939, Lachowicz studied at the State Academy of Plastic Arts in Warsaw. He also includes graphics, painting and drawing among his skills and his photography reflects his fine art background. He is President of the International Drawing Triennale in Warsaw, and has staged several major exhibitions in Poland.

38

GABRIEL CUALLADO

Young girl playing, Gandía, Valencia

Black-and-white/silver, 298mm x 442mm

Gabriel Cualladó was born in Valencia in 1925 and began to take photographs in 1950. For over forty years he has been a distinguished figure in Spanish photography, finding inspiration and subject matter in his native country. He has received several major commissions, including one from the French Department of Tourism; and has exhibited frequently in Spain, France and Holland.

39

ROBERTO KOCH

Park Avenue
From the series **Exit - Pictures from the United States**

Black-and-white/silver, 380mm x 255mm

Roberto Koch is founder of the Italian photo-agency, Contrasto, and has been a professional photographer since 1978. He has been a regular contributor to *Epoca, Stern, Time, Merian, The New York Times*, and other major publications. In 1988, he won the Kodak Award in Italy and had a major exhibition of work at Il Diaframma, Milan. He has recently undertaken projects in the USSR, and in the USA, celebrating 500 years of America.

40

GABOR KEREKES

Chiromancia/My Hand
From **The Phenomena of Nature**

Black-and-white/silver, 200mm x 260mm

Born in 1945, Gábor Kerekes was a waiter for nine years before becoming a photographer. He worked as a technical photographer at the Research Institute of the Iron Industry; but in his own private work, he increasingly sought to break with the traditional language of photography. He first exhibited in Budapest in 1973 and has participated in some fifty exhibitions in Hungary and abroad. The Hungarian journal *Photography* has awarded him prizes for excellence on ten occasions.

41

TONO STANO

Sharp Direction

Black-and-white/silver, 386mm x 496mm

Born in Moravia in 1960, Tono Stano studied at the School of Applied Arts, Bratislava and the FAMU Department of Photography, Prague. Part of the new wave of Czechoslovakian photographers, anticipating social change in Eastern Europe, he has worked as a freelance since 1986 and has exhibited in Prague, Germany, Italy and Great Britain.

42

ALFRED SEILAND

On the Green, Bramshaw, England, 1990

Colour, 295mm x 375mm

Alfred Seiland has been a freelance photographer in his native Austria since 1977. He works exclusively in colour and contributes to numerous magazines. His one-man exhibitions have toured in Austria, Switzerland, Germany, Italy and the USA; his work is in the Museum of Modern Art, New York; Museum of Fine Arts, Houston; the Bibliothèque Nationale, Paris; the Bundesministerium fur Unterricht und Kunst, Vienna, and many other collections. Publications include *East Coast - West Coast.*

43

MARINA COX

VI

From **Archeologies Deraisonnables**, 1992

Black-and-white/silver, 40cm x 50cm

Born in Sicily, Marina Cox now lives in Brussels, where she gained a masters degree in photography. Since 1986, she has had numerous exhibitions and publications in Europe, the USA and France. Her best-known series is **Souvenirs de Voyages** (1991); her submission for the ICI International Prize comes from its sequel.

44

MIRO SVOLIK

A Cross-country Run

Black-and-white/silver, 445mm x 618mm

Miro Svolík studied art photography in Prague and in 1989 won first prize in the International Photography Triennial, Essingen, Germany; the following year he won the ICP's sixth annual award for young photographers in New York; and in 1991, he was artist-in-residence to **Projects UK** in Newcastle-upon-Tyne.

45

YIORGOS DEPOLLAS

The Only Picture of Miss Suzan Scott's Kidnapping
From **Unpublished Documents**

Black-and-white/silver, 500mm x 600mm

Born in Athens in 1947, Depóllas followed an early spell in photography with work in cinematography. In 1975, he opened his own studio for fashion and commercial work; in 1979, with others, he created the 'Photography Centre of Athens' devoted to creative photography; and in the same year he also opened his own studio, 'Image'. He has exhibited in Europe and his photographs are in the Bibliothèque Nationale and Audiovisuel in Paris.

47

EDOUARD BOUBAT

Palais Royal Garden, Paris, June 1992

Black-and-white/silver, 245mm x 357mm

Born in 1923, Boubat started his photographic career with the French magazine *Realités*, after the Second World War. Initially known for his photo-essays from around the world, over the last decades, Boubat has concentrated on photographing in Paris with 'a keen eye for the bizarre quality and surrealism of simple everyday scenes'. He has exhibited widely, including major shows in the USA and Japan. In 1988, he won the Hasselblad Prize.

46

GERARD UFERAS

Glyndebourne
From **Backstage in European Opera Houses**

Black-and-white/silver, 305mm x 465mm

Uferas became a documentary photographer in 1984, contributing to *Liberation* newspaper, and in 1985 he helped found the agency Vu. He has worked in advertising, winning the 'Prix des Directeurs Artistique' in 1987; and in 1990, his project on opera houses in Europe was grant-aided by the French Ministry of Foreign Affairs. He has exhibited in Paris and Switzerland, and won the 1991 BP Arts Journalism Award.

48

JACQUES SONCK

Untitled

Black-and-white/ silver, 475mm x 475mm

Born in Ghent in 1949, Sonck studied photography at the Institute for Photography and Film, Brussels. Now resident Photographer at the Cultural Department of the Province of Antwerp, he has also established a reputation for portrait work. He has exhibited Holland, Germany, France and the USA, as well as in Belgium. His work is in collections in the Centre National de la Photographie, Paris and the Museum voor Fotografie, Antwerp.

49

JORGE MOLDER

From the series **Insomnia**

Black-and-white/silver, 260mm x 260mm

Jorge Molder was born in Lisbon in 1947. He studied philosophy but exhibited as a photographer for the first time in 1977. He has exhibited frequently in Portugal and abroad and his work is to be found in many collections, including the Fundaçao Calouste Gulbenkian and the Art Institute of Chicago.

51

GYORGY TOTH

Eszter

Black-and-white/silver, 470mm x 565mm

Currently working as a press photographer for Hungarian television, Tóth acknowledges the influence of Diane Arbus in his work. He has been a professional photographer for twenty years and used to publish a Hungarian edition of *Playboy*. He has exhibited regularly in Budapest since 1982, and his work has also toured to Paris, Prague and Amsterdam.

50

AD VAN DENDEREN

Acclimatisation-room: new miners are tested as to whether they can stand the underground heat
From **Black Labour in South Africa**

Black-and-white/silver, 310mm x 460mm

A freelance documentary photographer, Ad van Denderen was born in 1943; he has travelled widely in South Africa, Turkey and India covering social and political issues and contributes to the magazines *Avenue*, *Vrij Nederland*, *Stern* and *Geo*. He has exhibited in the Netherlands and Belgium, and in 1991 was awarded the Netherlands premier photography prize, the Alblas Award.

52

TUIJA LINDSTROM

From **The Girls at Bull's Pond**

Black-and-white/silver, 297mm x 305mm

Finnish-born, Tuija Lindström later moved to Sweden and studied at the GFU Photographic College and the School of Modern Arts in Stockholm. In 1988, she won Finland's major photography award, the Daniel Nyblin Prize. Her expressed ambition is to develop the photographic image as an art form, and she also lectures and teaches. Her work has been exhibited widely in Northern Europe.

53

PAUL DEN HOLLANDER

Untitled, 1992

Black-and-white/silver, 460mm x 460mm

A graduate of the Academy of Fine Arts in Breda, Paul den Hollander worked in farming for a spell before establishing himself as a photographer of place - both rural and urban. His work has been commissioned in many European countries, including France, Spain, Italy and Belgium; and major projects include **Moments in Time** and **Les Pyramides du Nord**.

54

GIOVANNI GASTEL

Ecological Tie

Colour, 406mm x 508mm

Born in 1955, Gastel was attracted early in life to the arts. In his teens, he studied experimental drama, and published a book of poems at the age of sixteen. Since 1981, he has worked as a photographer, first publishing in *Annabella* magazine, in that year. He has exhibited in Paris, Madrid and London; and has designed the visual image of several internationally-known corporations: Christian Dior, Guerlain, Nina Ricci, Krizia.

55

KJELL STEN TOLLEFSEN

Apartheid

Colour, 400mm x 400mm

Now nearly eighty years old, 'Kjell S' is unquestionably the senior entrant in the ICI Photography Awards. He started his career in photography quite late in life, in 1943, in an advertising agency in Oslo. He established a reputation for black-and-white work in the 1940s, but colour proved to be his medium. He contributes regularly to major photographic magazines and his photographs have been exhibited in Northern Europe, Spain and Los Angeles. He still photographs energetically and holds photography workshops.

56

LUC CHESSEX

New Delhi, India, 1990

Black-and-white/silver, 390mm x 570mm

Born and educated in Lausanne, Chessex studied photography in Vevey. He has been a freelance documentary photographer since 1959, working in Latin America in the early 1970s and in Africa for the Red Cross from 1978-80. He has also taught photography, and made films; his exhibitions have toured extensively in Europe and he has published six books of photographic work.

57

STEFAN MOSES

Farm labour becomes mechanised, Neukirchen, Wyhra, 1990

Black-and-white/silver, 430mm x 550mm

Born in 1928, Stefan Moses has had a distinguished career as a major figure on the German photographic scene, contributing to *Stern* magazine, and other major publications for over four decades. His individual style - neither photo-reporter nor 'art' photographer - crosses the boundaries of photographic convention. He has exhibited throughout the world; and in 1988, was awarded the Kodak Photo Book Prize.

58

SERGEI GITMAN

People at Meeting
From **Memorial Meeting in Tbilisi, Georgia, 9 April, 1990**

Colour, 300mm x 400mm

Born in Moscow in 1944, Sergei Gitman worked as a translator for thirteen years, but in the mid-eighties started to turn increasingly to photography. He is a perceptive documentary photographer and in 1988, he set up FotoMost, an agency for photographic exchanges with other countries. His work is included in the collections of the Pushkin Museum of Fine Arts, Moscow; Museum of Modern Art, New York; and the Bibliothèque Nationale, Paris.

59

NADEZDA CHIPEVA

The Flush

Colour, 180mm x 260mm

Nadezda Chipeva was born in Sofia where she also studied photography, graduating in 1983. She has maintained an independent documentary eye, combining her own freelance photography with laboratory work in the Bulgarian News Agency. She has won several awards, has exhibited in Bulgaria and regularly contributes to magazines and newspapers.

60

NIKOS ECONOMOPOULOS

Main market in the old town, Korce, 1990
From the series **Balkan Man**

Black-and-white/silver, 610mm x 760mm

Nikos Econompoulos was born in Greece in 1953. After studying at the University of Parma in Italy, he worked as a journalist in Greece for eight years. In 1988, he chose photography as his career, working with *Camera International*; he has also worked on a long term personal project called **Balkan Man**. In 1990, he was invited to join Magnum Photos; and in 1991, he was a finalist in the Henri Cartier-Bresson Award in Paris. He has exhibited in Greece and Italy.

THE PHOTOGRAPHERS